Amour Fou
by Stacie Seidl

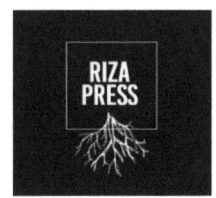

Amour Fou

Copyright © 2019 by Stacie Seidl
All rights reserved. No part of this publication may be reproduced, distributed, or transmitted in any form or by any means, including photocopying, recording, or other electronic or mechanical methods, without the prior written permission of the publisher, except in the case of brief quotations embodied in critical reviews and certain other noncommercial uses permitted by copyright law.

First Printing, 2020
Printing information available on the last page.

ISBN (sc) 978-1-989795-01-9
ISBN (e) 978-1-989795-02-6

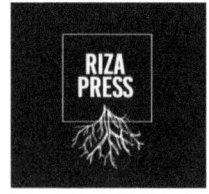

Illustrator: Ava Balis
Riza Publishing Press
Ottawa, ON, Canada
www.rizapress.com

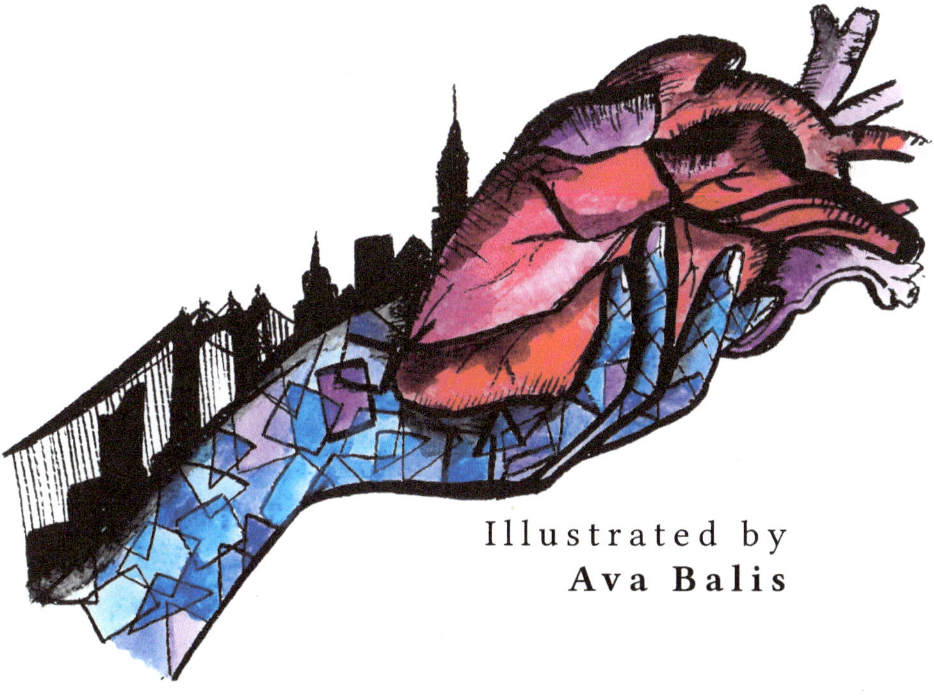

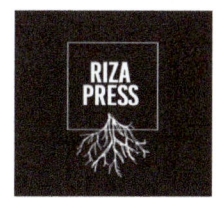

Illustrated by
Ava Balis

part one:
Amour

MOMENTS

I've learned to make the most of the moments
Though few and far between
They linger
Imprinting
Reminding
When it's real it's forever

SOULSTRUCK

I often catch myself wishing
Our souls had found each other
Many moons ago
So that I might have loved you longer

But then my heart beats softly
Reminding me that
I have loved you always
Long before the mind can comprehend

PEACE

When you hold me in your arms
The rest of the world fades away
The rage inside me calms
The stress begins to wane
In case you didn't know it
You've saved me with your love
Made me smile with your wit
You fit me like a glove
We have the world at our feet
And I can't wait to start
Next to you I am complete
Mind, body, soul, and heart

BONDED

A bond so deep
It's not broken by
Time, space or the choices we make
A love so real
It cannot be explained, understood or matched
Like a magnet I'm drawn
To your spirit, your energy
It captures my soul lighting it on fire
I lose myself in every moment
My will powerless against your touch
The smell of your skin
Your lips on mine
Ecstasy in its purest form

Stacie Seidl

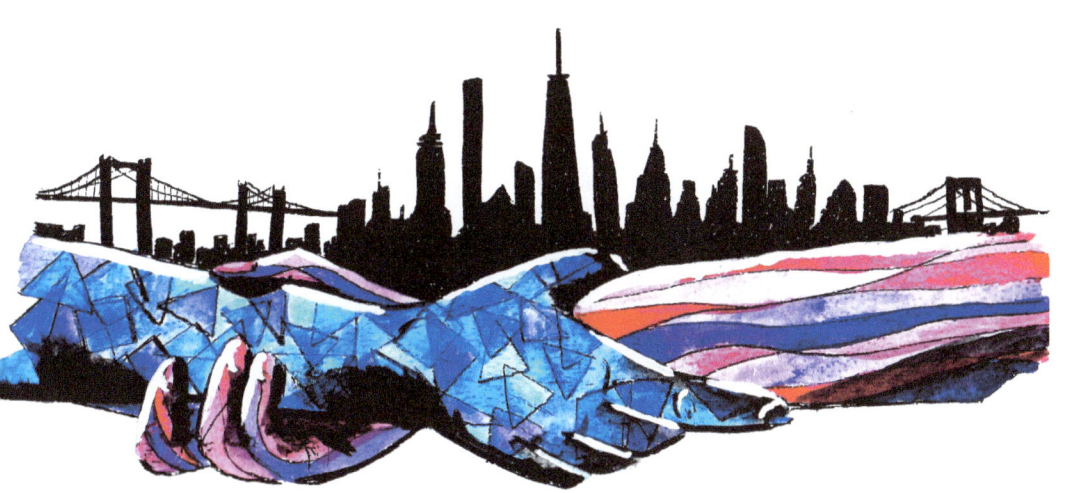

Amour Fou

DIVINE

When the sky goes dark infinitely
And the sun refuses to shine
Let my love radiate through you intimately
And show you a glimpse of the divine

Stacie Seidl

TIPSY

The echo of the sound
Of my heart pounding in my chest
Has got me feeling tipsy
A fire burning in my breast
I can't believe I'm doing this
After all the time gone by
My broken heart alive again
His love has got me high
Flying above the limit
Never wanting to come down
Together I'm in ecstasy
Of this beautiful love we've found

Amour Fou

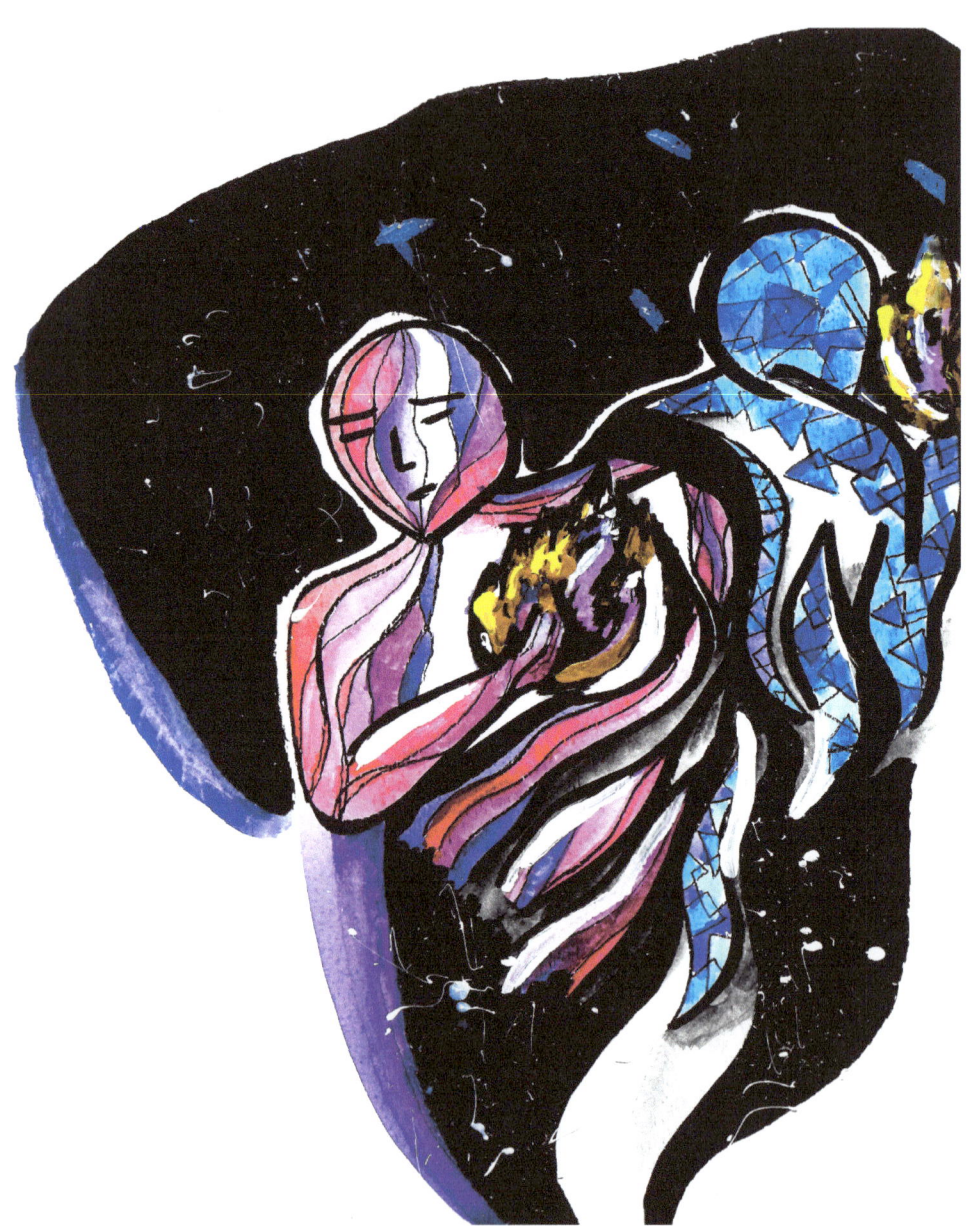

Stacie Seidl

BURN

I truly don't know what to make of it
So instead I'll just let it burn
Not worry about putting the fire out
Allow the love to return
Its shape an unrecognizable lifeform
That no one else can perceive
A dream I've seen over and over again
A love my heart cannot leave

UNEXPECTED

Words cannot explain it
Something has come over me
Changing the way I had expected every situation to turn out

A love so strong it leaves me weak
I see no one else
Nothing can touch us

A little piece of heaven here on Earth
My heart is full
Every beat sends happiness racing through my veins

Doubts have disappeared
I know you are meant for me
Together forever is no longer out of my reach

Everything I ever wanted
Dreamed about
Cried out for

All at once has swept me off my feet
My smile is real now
My goals suddenly within my reach

The darkness has faded
The pain is gone
Vanished almost like it never was

Stacie Seidl

KINDRED

When the one you love
Is your very best friend
You can tell each other anything
Without having to pretend
Love on another level
Beyond superficial demand
Something like nothing else
Kindred souls understand
There is nothing that compares
Even to the worst days
A connection that defies the odds
Disproves all the clichés
Its value forever underrated
In a world full of instant gratification
To me a sacred gift
That needs no explanation

Amour Fou

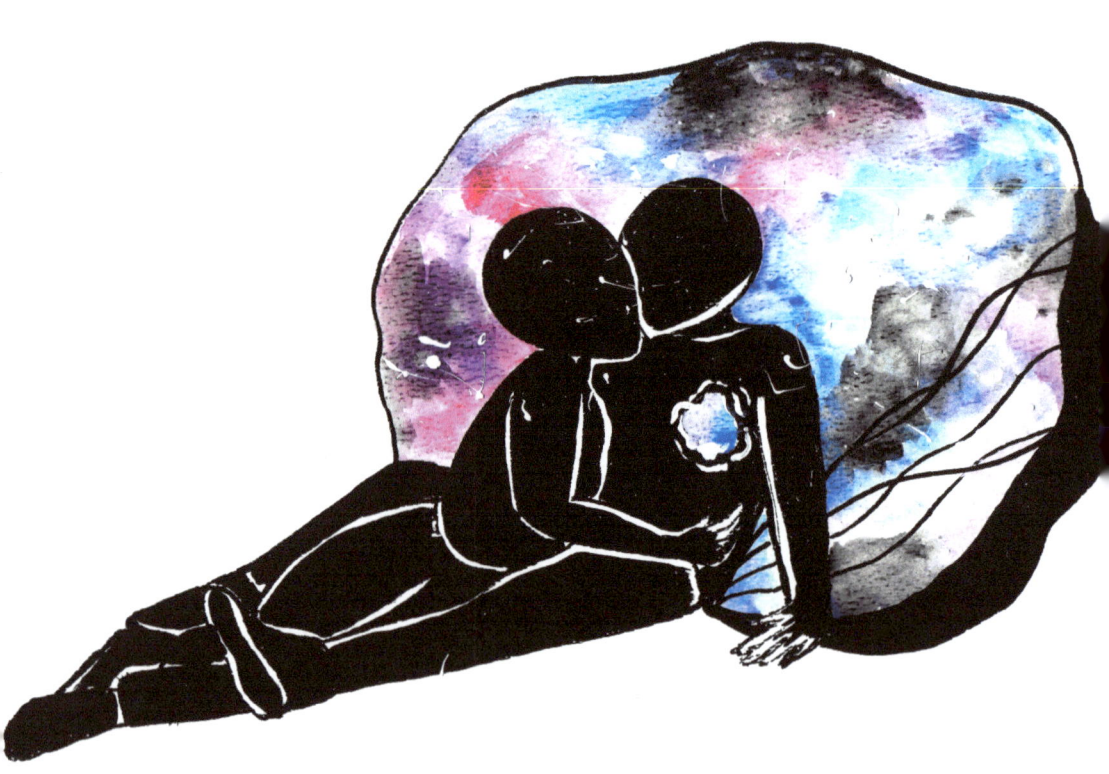

Stacie Seidl

CONTINUUM

No matter what
Until her lungs quit breathing air
He will be the one
To which no one else compares
He will be the one
Her heart continuously calls
Never can be done
Over and over again she falls

REMAINS

Intensely
Almost more than she could take
He loved her deeply
Making it hard for them to break
In spite of all the starts and stops
Their hearts remained connected
A bond that could not be swapped
Even when they both neglect it

Stacie Seidl

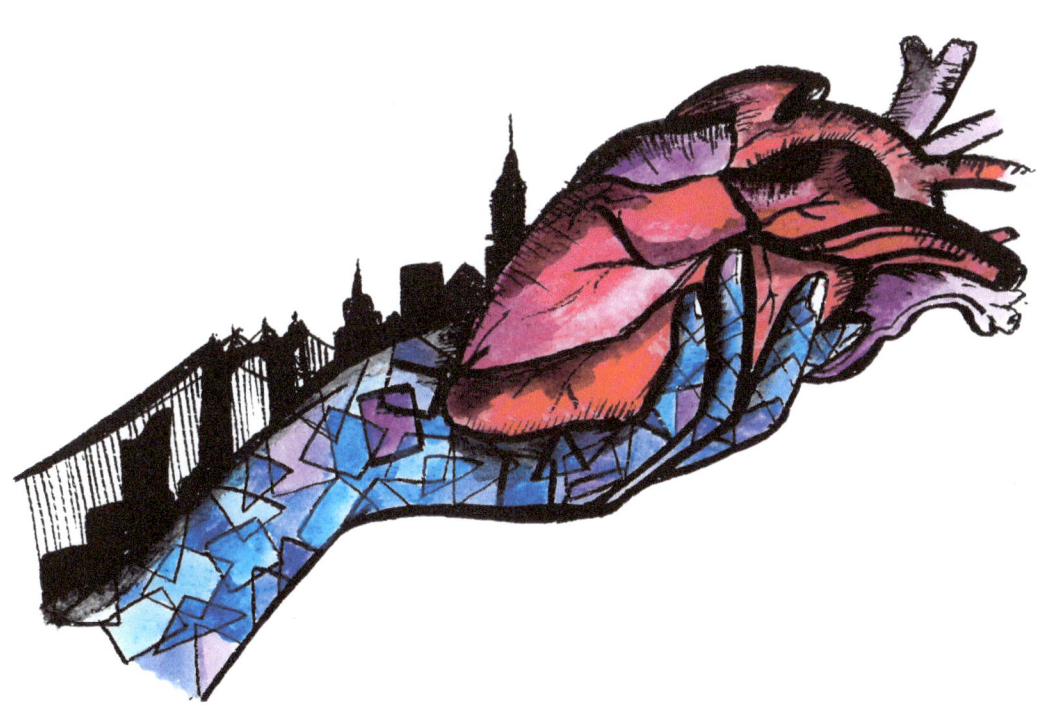

Amour Fou

ESSENCE

It's the way
That your essence caresses me
Like a lover's fingertips on my skin
Enveloping all of my senses
Touching me deep within

Stacie Seidl

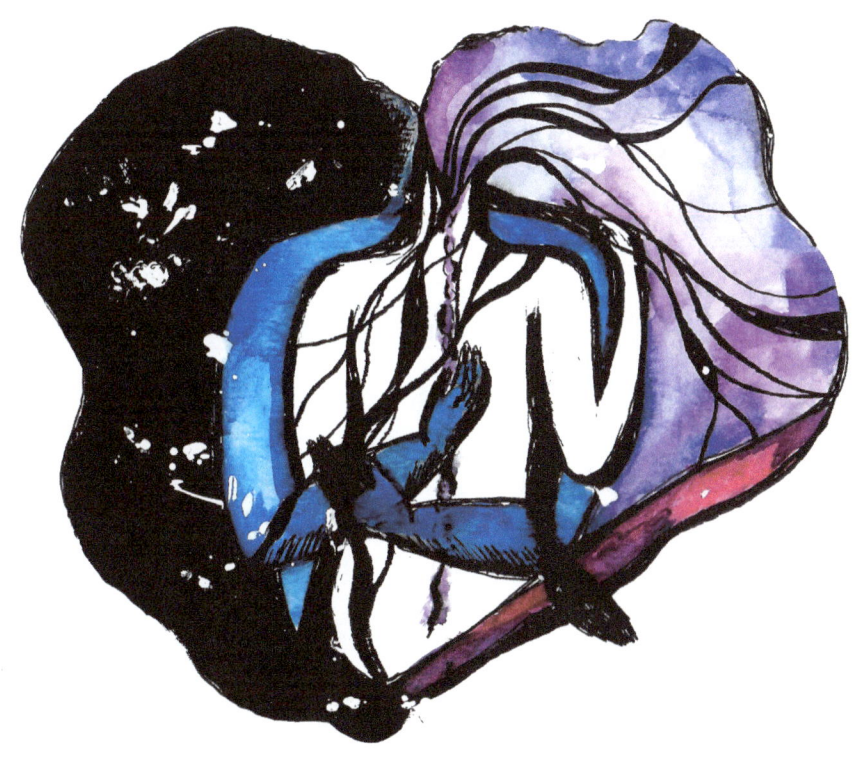

Amour Fou

BLESSED

Selfishly I rejoice
At the news I've longed to hear
Suddenly returning choice
That never before was there
A day that I have dreamed of
Unexpectedly arrives
Free to give our love
Somehow we survived
The next chapter of the story
Reveals the unforeseen
Released from purgatory
No longer in between

UNDENIABLE

The delayed reaction of these tears is so surprising. There was a time when I couldn't hold them back at even just the thought of him leaving again. It's all changed now. What deep down I knew I no longer have to question. Love is undeniable and I feel it as soon as he looks in my direction. That almost reverent way he lets himself back into my mind and body. The way he touches me in places no other man ever will. Perhaps it is because I'm blessed with this part of him that I no longer cry. Wishes for what we don't have lay waste to the beauty of what we share. His arms around me shut out everything less.

Amour Fou

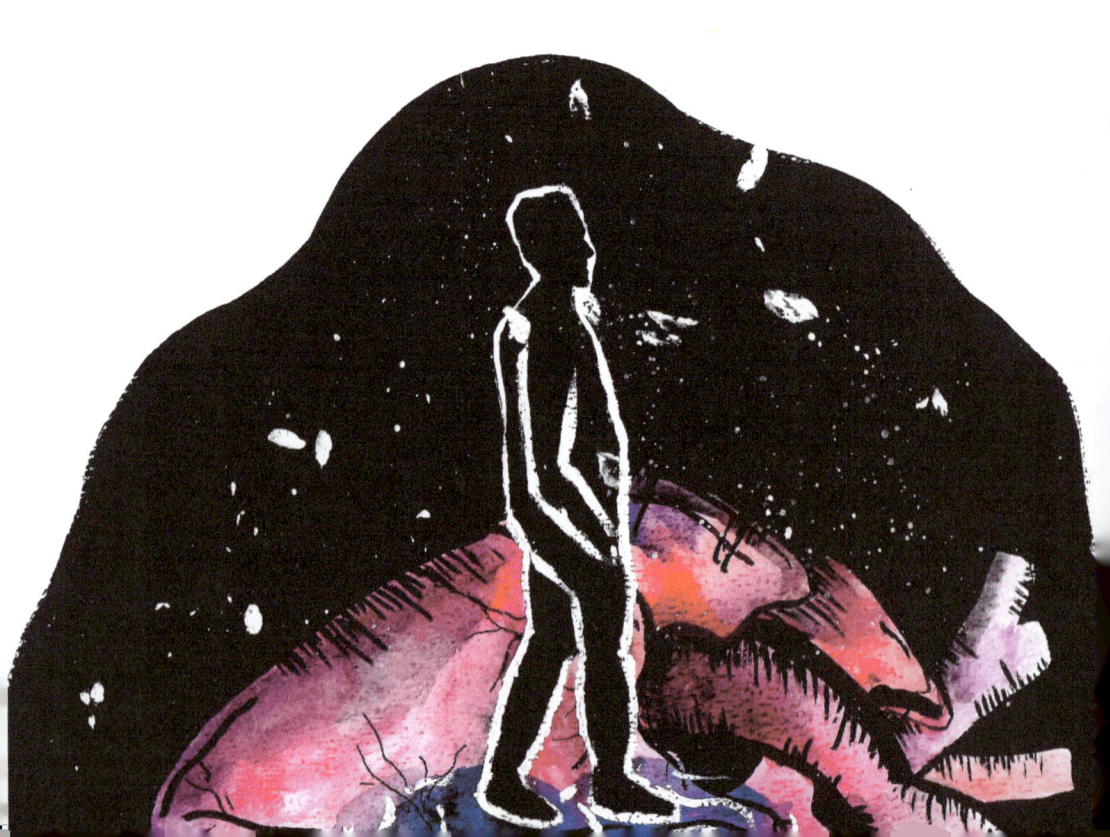

part two:
Fou

Stacie Seidl

TEMPEST

The anger ebbs and flows
like the raging ocean during a hurricane
Smashing and destroying everything it comes close to
Then suddenly calming so foolish hearts
expose their vulnerability
Time after time
As if no lesson is learned at all
The storm will return
Knocking down everything love recklessly built
Insanely believing one more time that forever could actually
endure the furious tempest of her heart

MASQUERADE

What I thought we were
has turned into a masquerade ball
it seems that only I forgot to dress up for
My mask once so beautiful
Has become tattered and torn
No longer creating
the illusion so carefully crafted
Myself instead all there is to see

INTUITION

I've spent so much time
Hanging in the balance
Between almost and not yet
Waiting for a time
That I knew in my heart
Would never come for us
Intuition so often ignored
When stacked against
Benefit of the doubt

DEVOID

It only took 2 weeks and 2 days this time
Until he returned her heart
to its most uncomfortable state
The place he always leaves it
Without any appearance of a care or feeling
Left with a simple message devoid of any detail
Closed with an xoxo like it was the end of a good morning text
and not yet another chance
that she shouldn't have given
Like it was so easy
Like her heart wasn't being ripped painfully from its cage
inducing the sadness that always wins
Like the aftermath didn't matter
When she would have died for him

Stacie Seidl

WORTHY

She refused to be
just another beautiful heart he had collected
Refused to hide her cracks
to be worthy of a place on display
She was not like the rest and he knew it
That's why he kept running away

Amour Fou

TWISTED

"But it's you that I love," he screams
As his actions decry the words
Must have had it twisted
The meaning became blurred
"You know how I feel", he says
As he refuses to show & prove
Fooled me once again
My love I must remove

Stacie Seidl

BATED

There was a time when we were so in sync
What's becoming a distant memory
I don't know how to let go of
Even as I begin to forget your face
The sound of your voice
The way that loving you touched me so deeply
I mourn the loss of what we almost were
Always waiting with bated breath
For the moment of your return
Foolishly refusing to give up the hope
that you will love me again like you almost did
Chasing it like a designer drug meant to leave me
forever on the cusp of the best high of my life

Amour Fou

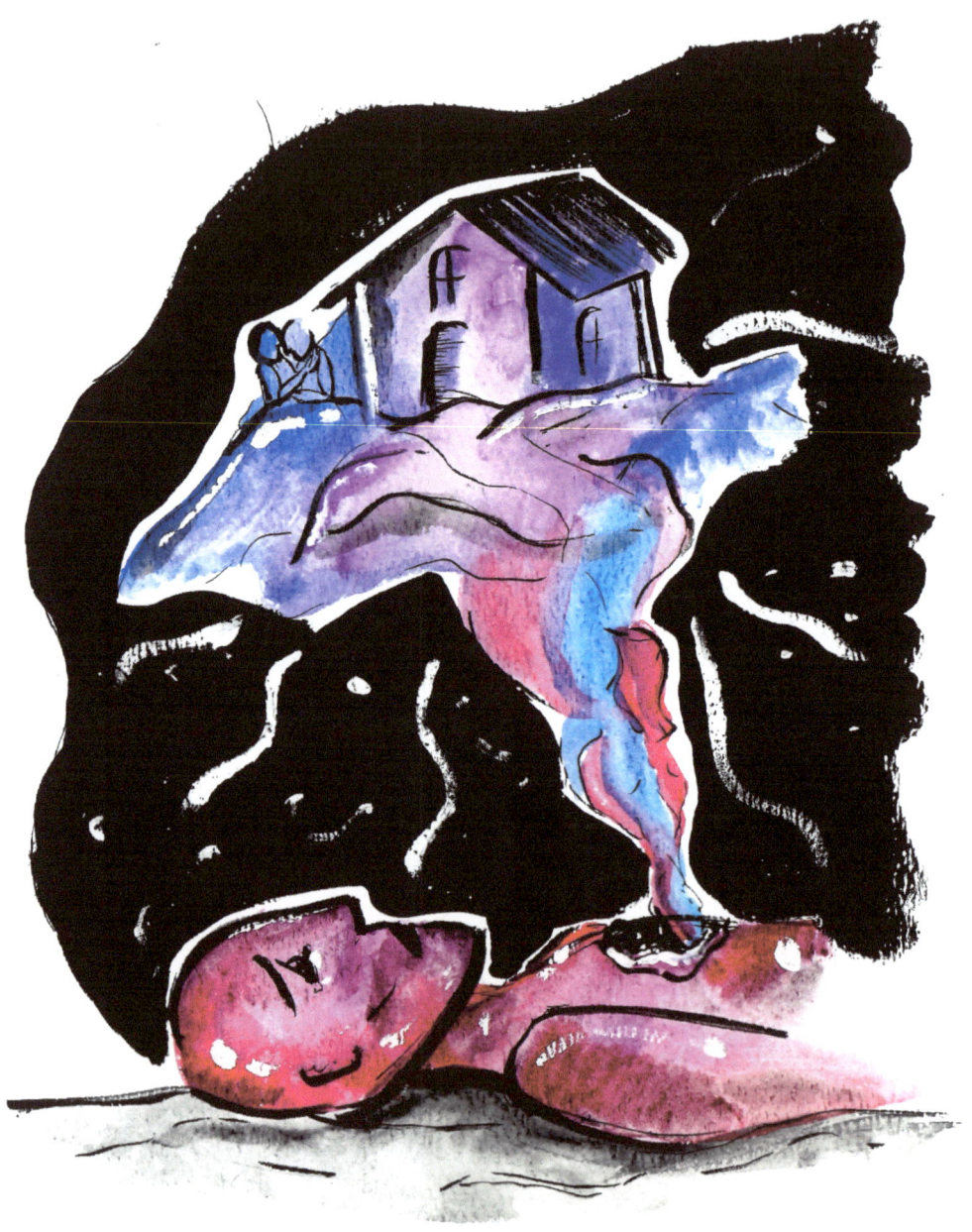

Stacie Seidl

ILLUSION

I had my chance to walk away clean
But I gave it up in favor of living
in the filthy illusion he had created
with words I had dreamed of hearing
since the day we met
Always followed up with half-hearted attempts
at fulfilling their promises
Never enough
Over time I began to realize the deception
A typical story I swore I'd never fall for
Until I was choosing it over and over again
Afraid to give up
what was never mine in the first place
Terrified to be without him

Amour Fou

SPINNING

He and I could never find
Common ground to stand on
Chose instead to run and hide
Broken hearts marathon
Slowly spinning in circles
Unable to just let go
Losing hope for a miracle
Abandonment vertigo

Stacie Seidl

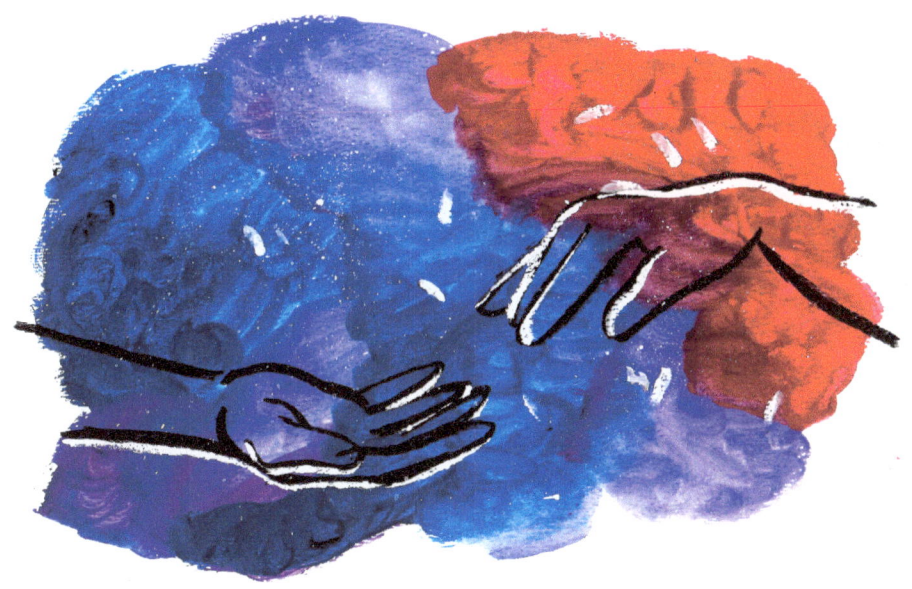

Amour Fou

TEMPORARY

He was only here temporarily
To teach you again
what you should have already known
It wasn't meant to be
Sad and contrite as it sounds
It's time to say goodbye
Love did a long time ago

CHASING

Part of me wishes that I had listened
When you so eloquently told me
That your heart would never be mine
Maybe then I wouldn't have spent the last 5 years
Chasing a ghost who only appears
To steal another piece of my soul
Then vanish again
As if my love wasn't home enough to stay
You lied to yourself as much as me
Thinking you could convince us both
That this thing of ours wasn't real
Some days I desperately want to believe you
But what else will give my heart life?

REALIZATION

Letting go of the person you love
Of all the dreams and hopes you kept tucked away
in the corners of your broken heart
The realization that you were just one of the many
beautiful faces he chose to surround himself with
Gazing through the false partition
you didn't even know you had been hiding behind
Finally choosing self

Stacie Seidl

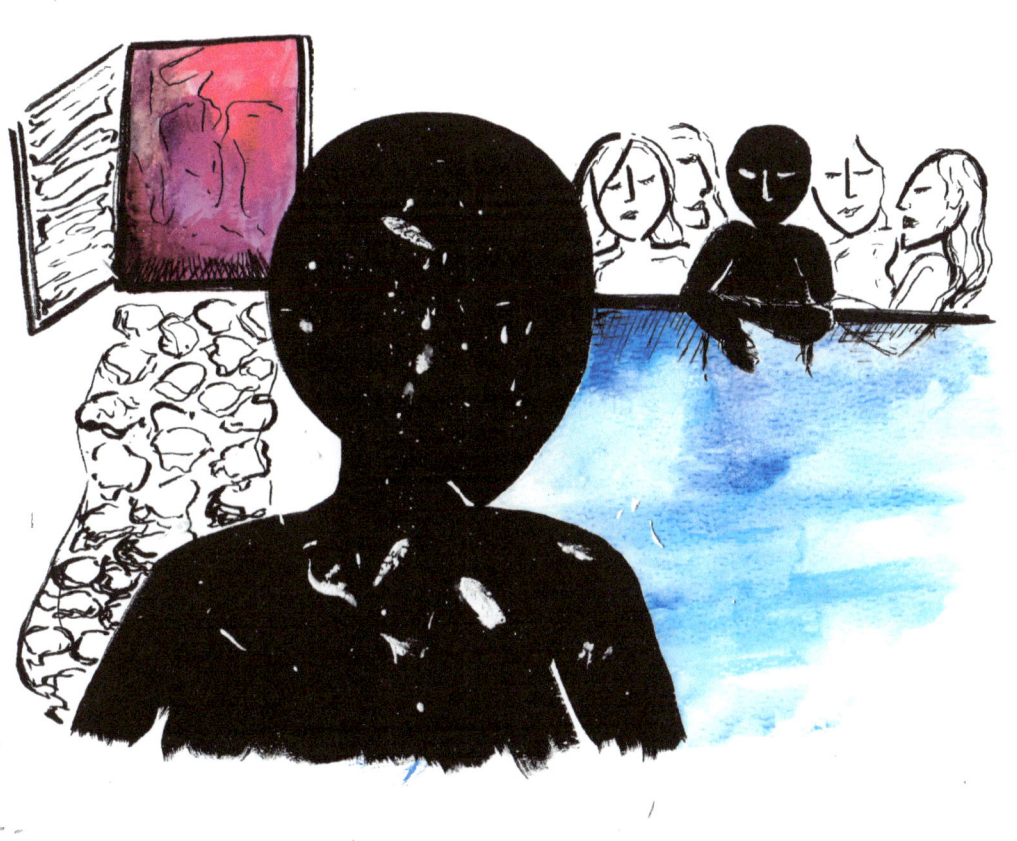

Amour Fou

CODEPENDENT

When tears stay hovering at the surface
Welling up at the most random moments
Wanting to cry your heart out
But the dam only breaks for a second
When every beat of your heart aches
Slow motion as it breaks
Desperately needing a way out
But so comfortably codependent

Stacie Seidl

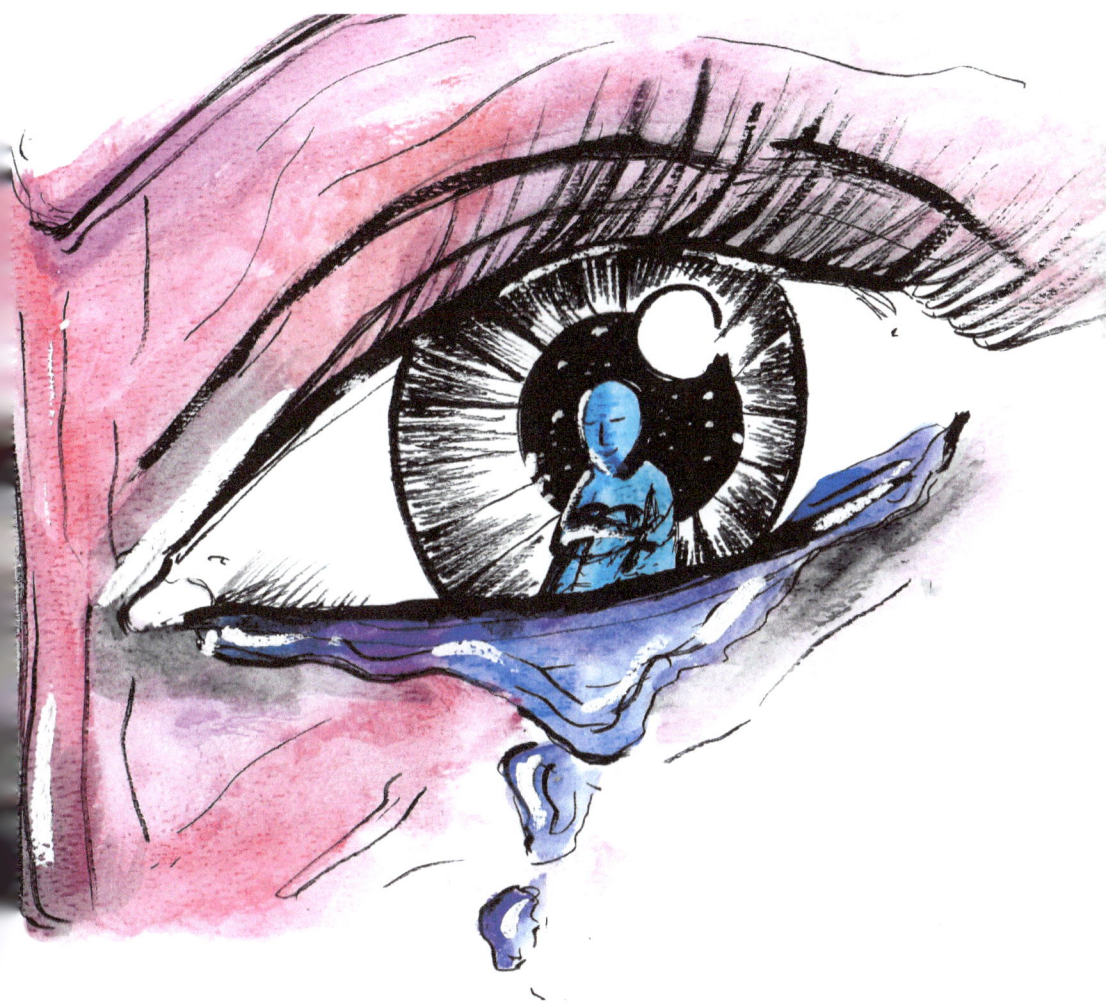

PHANTOM

Our love is like a ghost
A phantom limb that I still feel
An addict overdosed
Open wounds that just won't heal
Our love sustains my life
While slowly taking it away
Its cost a heavy price
I alone have to pay

Stacie Seidl

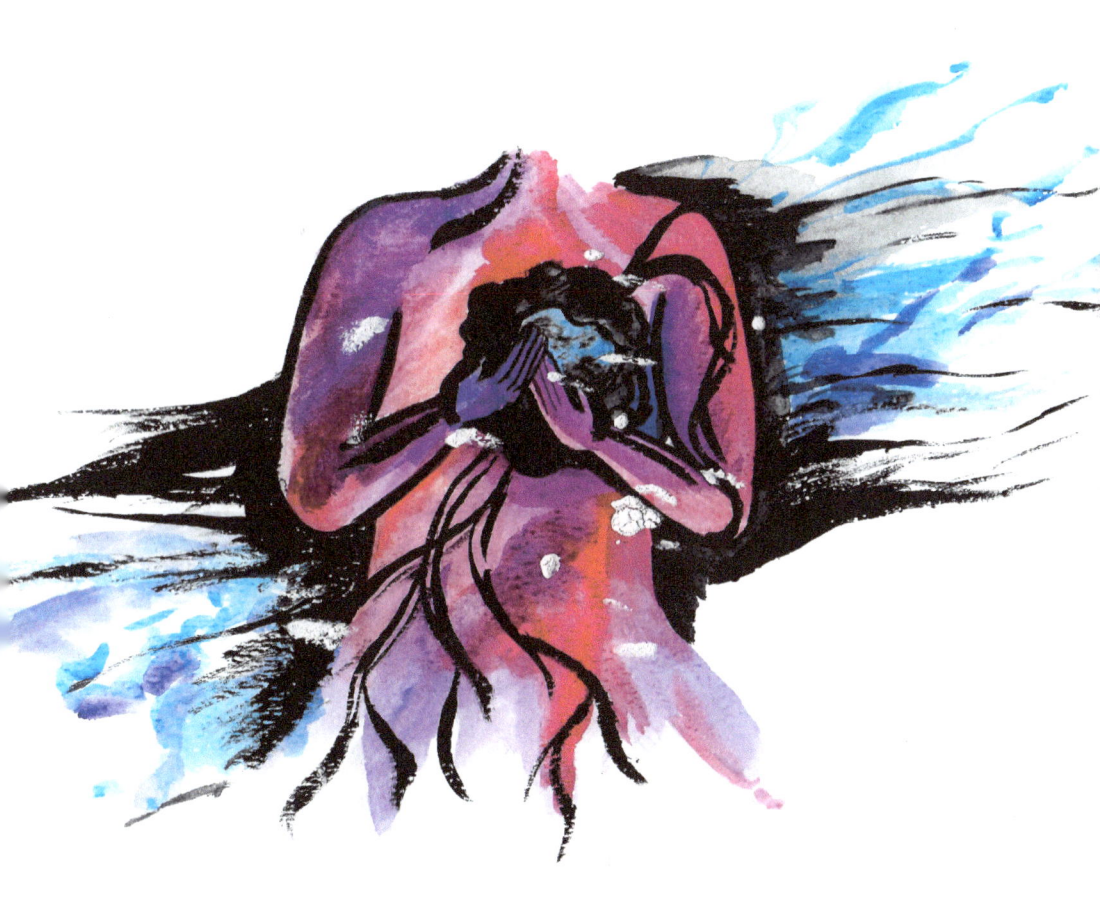

RELEASED

When finally I am over you I see it all so clear. The blinders my heart pulled over my eyes are lifted.
The holds on my love released
No malice, hate, or regrets left to haunt me
Free
Strong
Moving on

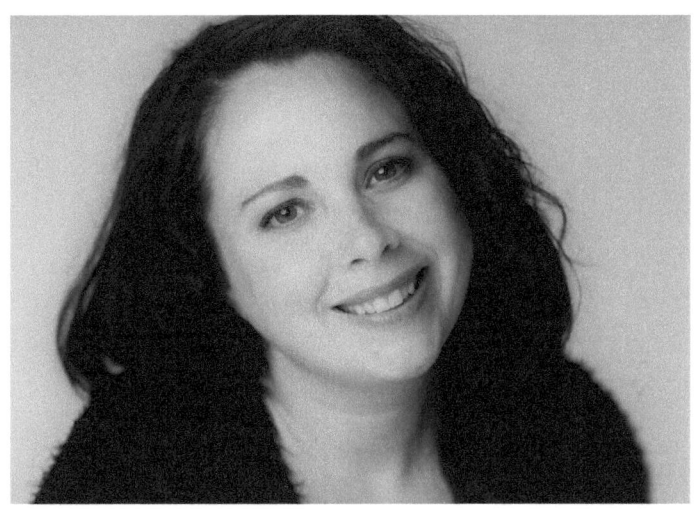

ABOUT THE AUTHOR

Stacie Seidl is a writer, poet and author living in Queens New York. Her first book, *Breathing Underwater*, was published in 2016. She was also published in *Mosaic: A Collection from the Instagram Community* in 2019. The chapbook chronicles through words her lifelong struggle with PTSD, Panic Disorder, and Depression. She has continued to write on a variety of topics and was recently inducted into the International English Honor Society, Sigma Tau Delta. Stacie writes in the hope that her words will reach those who are out there suffering, and they will find solace in knowing they are not alone.

PRAISE FOR AMOUR FOU

"From blinding love and happiness through to heartbreak and realisation, Armour Fou takes the reader on an emotional and relatable journey through one of the most complicated feelings in life; love. For anyone seeking reassurance that they are not alone, or looking for solace and peace within the pages of a beautiful book, these words promise comfort and wisdom. The author has a talent of weaving poetry and prose in a manner of art, and the combination of perfectly rhyming poetry with story telling prose is testimony to her brilliant, rising talent. A thoroughly enjoyable and cozy read with some stunning illustrations to boot. From the moment I turned the first page, I knew I wasn't alone.."
    - Gemma Marie, author of *The Anatomy of Wanting*

"I found in Stacie Seidl's words a profound, and courageous confession. Her relatable words touch the bottom of our hearts, disarming our delusions, and expectations. These poems are an exquisite reminder that the best of us is yet to come, and that love can be a part of it."
    - Ruben Ramires, poet and illustrator

"Stacie's collection is a timeless piece centered around an age-old idea, but spun tenderly into something entirely its own. Her writing takes you through the ebb and flow of love, heartache, and the healing that comes, sometimes, much later."
    - Beth Huston, Founder of Pen & Pendulum

www.ingramcontent.com/pod-product-compliance
Lightning Source LLC
Chambersburg PA
CBHW041218070526
44583CB00006B/171